# Remote Auditing

Other Paton Professional Books by Denise Robitaille:

- *The Corrective Action Handbook, Second Edition*
- *The Preventive Action Handbook, Second Edition*
- *The Management Review Handbook, Second Edition*
- *Document Control*
- *Root Cause Analysis*
- *9 Keys to Successful Audits*
- *The (Almost) Painless ISO 9001:2015 Transition*
- *Managing Supplier-Related Processes*

Order these and other titles online at:
www.patonprofessional.com.

# Remote Auditing

A QUICK AND EASY GUIDE
FOR MANAGEMENT SYSTEM AUDITORS

## Denise Robitaille

PROFESSIONAL

Houston

Most Paton Professional books are available at quantity discounts when purchased in bulk. For more information, contact:

Paton Professional
Email: *books@patonprofessional.com*
Web: *www.patonprofessional.com*

ISBN: 978-1-932828-31-3

# Contents

*To my darlings Brooke and Paige who keep their Mémère smiling when the audits take me far from home.*

# CHAPTER 1

# Introduction

Remote auditing has been around for well over a decade. Its popularity has been spurred by advances in technology and the globalization of economies. There has been an uptick in multi-site companies with operations scattered across the map and more small and medium-size enterprises engaged in international commerce. Both the types of organizations and the modes of conducting business have evolved as global transportation and information and communication technology (ICT) have become more ubiquitous and reliable. Web-based portals facilitate procurement and shipping processes. Container ships have grown so large the Panama Canal had to be widened. Artificial intelligence has moved from the realm of science fiction to the manufacturing floor.

The recent impetus for remote auditing has catapulted the practice into the forefront of audit community dialogue. It's essential to ensure that this escalation of off-site assessments does not result in a dissolution of the integrity of conformity assessment. This alternate method does not diminish the need to ensure organizational conformance to requirements. Audits still need to be conducted. There is still a need to assess affiliate companies, branch locations, and potential suppliers.

The big change is that now there are many more organizations—both customers and suppliers—that are geographically distant. Third-party certification audits can now cover sites on several continents. The constraints this presents relate primarily to time and travel expenditures. Remote auditing can bring more efficiency to an audit program because the technology that supports it is exponentially more affordable and available than it was even ten years ago.

The challenge presented by the 2020 COVID-19 pandemic added another compelling argument to make the shift to remote auditing activities: the need to protect individuals and communities from the transmission of a deadly virus.

The purpose of auditing is to verify the conformance of an organization's processes and management system to defined requirements. Depending on the type of audit and the objective, the conformance criteria vary. The standard against which an audit may be conducted could be an organization's own procedures and documented requirements; a management system standard such as ISO 9001, AS9100, or IATF 16949; customer-specified requirements; or government regulations such as those put forth by the Food and Drug Administration, Federal Aviation Administration, or Nuclear Regulatory Commission.

Audits should result in:

- Qualification (or continued approval) of suppliers
- Fulfillment of customer requirements
- Continued certification to the ISO standard (or sector-specific equivalent)
- Improvements

Even with the constraints of remote auditing, these results still need to be achieved. Audits help us to identify problems, risks, good practices, and opportunities to better serve our customers. The information gathered from well-conducted audits is a company asset. The way the organization values and uses this asset is partially dependent on how audits are performed. Therefore, it is appropriate to develop tools and methods that allow for the continued ability to implement and maintain effective audit programs.

This book deals with the various aspects of remote auditing, including planning, risk assessment, logistical constraints, conducting the audit, and providing an informative audit report.

# CHAPTER 2

# Remote Auditing Overview

R emote auditing is a misnomer. It suggests that a new category of auditing has been created. In fact, it's merely the application of new tools and methods to the audit process. Remote audits involve the application of technology to gather information when in-person methods are not possible or desired. The level of sophistication of the technology can vary. It can run the gamut from simple phone calls and emails to video conferencing software and sharing of cloud-based documentation. The term "remote auditing" encompasses activities that facilitate the assessment of processes occurring in a location other than where the auditor is situated, using verification means that do not include face-to-face meetings. ISO 19011, Guidelines for auditing management systems, repeatedly refers to "remote audit activities."

The tools and methods may be different, but the same audit requirements apply. Auditors must assess if the auditee has determined inputs to processes, conducted activities under controlled conditions, provided the necessary support resources, defined the interrelation to other processes, ensured control throughout the process, verified the outcome, and retained requisite records and information relating to both the implementation of the activities and the verification of the product (or process output).

That having been said, for the sake of brevity and to mitigate ambiguity, we'll refer to the methods and activities as "remote audits" throughout this book. The basic elements of a remote audit are:

- Activities occur at a location other than where the auditor is situated regardless of the distance.
- There is no face-to-face meeting or on-site presence.
- The principles of auditing still apply.
- Same process; same requirements; different tools and methods.

It is possible to have an audit where some processes are assessed remotely while others are audited on-site. The advisability of conducting audits that combine both methods would be based on considerations that will be discussed in later chapters dealing with risk and planning.

## Differentiating from Virtual Auditing

Virtual auditing (another misnomer) is often confused with remote auditing. Virtual auditing refers to the auditing of virtual processes: That is processes that take place in a virtual environment. These are processes that occur without direct human intervention.

The concept of "virtual" reflects that which lacks geographic and tactile attributes. We cannot "locate" the object, see it with the naked eye, or come into physical contact with it. Nonetheless, those bytes of streaming data and documented information provide two things: implementation (and control) of processes through the execution of programs based on human-created algorithms and evidence of fulfillment of requirements. Examples include automated procurement based on ERP programs, e-commerce, and software-driven statistical process control performing both monitoring and readjustment of parameters of production machinery in real time.

Auditing virtual processes means that you can assess the integrity and completeness of the data that supports the automated outputs. An auditor should be able to assess the inputs, the risks, the support resources, and the control of the outputs.

Virtual processes or activities may be within the scope of a remote audit. For example, an auditor may be utilizing a web-sharing platform such as Skype. The auditee logs in and shares the desktop. As the auditor asks questions about the process, the auditee can click into the various programs to demonstrate how the virtual process is conducted and controlled.

---

# Benefits

Utilizing remote auditing manages a whole variety of constraints. By auditing processes remotely an organization may achieve immediate financial benefits. There are no travel expenses—no airfare, no hotel and meal costs, and no mileage compensation. It's an easy win. For third-party assessments, the client organization (auditee) often assumes the burden of paying travel expenses. They just roll it up into the cost of their certification. If part or all the initial registration and surveillance audits are conducted remotely, there is a proportionate cost saving to the overall maintenance of their ISO 9001 (or comparable) certificate.

Beyond the immediate financial boost there are other potential benefits to be derived.

There's greater flexibility in the quantity of audits to be completed because they consume fewer resources. An auditor doesn't spend hours or days traveling so there are more auditor hours available to apply directly to the audit process. Let's assume that a supplier audit takes six hours to complete and an auditor spends a total of eight hours traveling to and from the audit site. (In this hypothetical scenario the suppliers are all relatively local—within a few hours' drive of the company). If the audit is conducted remotely, most of those eight hours are now available for conducting other audits. (The whole eight hours aren't available because there will be time required to address telecommunication protocols and technology access issues). The time required to generate the audit report isn't shortened, because the report must contain all the same content as for an audit done on-site. Therefore, if you have 12–14 extra unassigned hours every month, it means that over the course of the year, there are approximately 150 more hours available to conduct additional audits. Under normal conditions, allowing for some variation in time, that means there are resources available to conduct an additional 15–

18 audits each year. Or, if the person conducting the audits has other respon-
sibilities, the time resource can be reallocated to other internal activities.

An alternative scenario dealing with a supplier auditing program could
have an even greater financial impact. Imagine that the company manufactures a complex medical device. Multiple components have critical attributes
and/or elaborate production and test protocols. The company has determined that the 20 level-one critical suppliers are to be audited twice per year.
The suppliers are scattered around the globe. If even one-third of the audits
could be conducted remotely, the cost savings could easily exceed $20,000–
$30,000 each year.

Add to this benefit the potential to broaden the pool of potential auditors.
There may be some well-qualified individuals who are unable to travel due to
family constraints. This provides them with an opportunity to develop their
auditor skills while augmenting the audit resources available to the company.

An organization with a multi-site scheme could choose to conduct some
of their internal audits remotely. They would experience the benefit of observing remote processes, such as quoting, from the customers' perspective,
and identifying possible risks and constraints in the process. Questions that
could arise include:

- How accessible is our product information on the website?
- What might cause a delay if a customer needs to change an order?
- How robust are our security protocols when customers send us CAD files?

It would be enlightening to observe how some of these contingencies are
managed when the person with the answer isn't in the next office.

Finally, as we all move inexorably into the digital age, it will be beneficial
to observe the level of agility our own organization and our suppliers have
with electronic media and virtual processes. From an internal audit perspective, it could detect risks for top management to consider. During supplier
audits it could identify those companies with a sustained and long-term commitment to improvement and innovation. And, for certification assessments
it could facilitate determining if, for example, an organization is effectively
managing technological changes that affect their ability to fulfill their customers' expectations.

# CHAPTER 3

# Identifying and Managing Risk

There are multiple and varied risks associated with conducting audits remotely. This doesn't mean that the method should not be undertaken or that the output would be inferior. Organizations should expect the same level of value regardless of the methods used to conduct the audits. As with any other process, it's important to identify and assess the risks and determine the appropriate course of action. The response to identified risks may involve changing how an audit is conducted, rescheduling, or deciding that a remote audit for certain processes or locations is not a viable option.

There are risks associated with any kind of audit method. On-site audits carry risks associated with physical harm, security breaches, and limited access to processes or evidence. Risks need to be determined and managed. In each instance, it's appropriate to begin by understanding the status quo—the current operating conditions. From this vantage point it's possible to determine what could go wrong. This provides the foundation to better assess risks and decide what can be done.

## Assessing Feasibility and Constraints

We begin by understanding the current processes and the environment in which the organization operates.

Considerations include:

- Number of auditors available:
  - o Adequate training in remote auditing activities
  - o Familiarity and agility with remote technology

- Quantity of audits within the scope of the audit plan or schedule
- Available technology:
  - o Teleconferencing
  - o Video conferencing and web-based meeting platforms
  - o File sharing programs
  - o Browser speed and bandwidth

- Customer or industry security constraints:
  - o International Traffic in Arms Regulations (ITAR) requirements that prohibit reproduction of documents
  - o Customer confidentiality contracts
  - o Password protected portals

- Environment:
  - o Appropriate space to accommodate online interviews:
    - ▪ Privacy and confidentiality
    - ▪ Distraction free

  - o Special environments, such as clean rooms
  - o Audits that include visits to customer sites such as for equipment installation

Once you understand the resources and constraints you can begin to identify the risks. Each risk can be related back to one or more of the considerations previously listed. What follows are some of the risks associated with remote auditing. The sequence that follows is not hierarchical and does not reflect prioritization or level of criticality.

# Risks

## Not being able to achieve audit objective

The audit objective relates to what you wish to achieve. Depending on the type of audit, there are several possibilities. These are examples of audit objectives:

- First-party audit (internal audits):
  - Determine conformance to management systems requirements such as ISO 9001, AS9100, IATF 16949, etc.
  - Identify problems and risks.
  - Assess effectiveness of implemented corrective action.
  - Discover opportunities to improve.

- Second-party audit (supplier audits):
  - Determine conformance to defined criteria (their own quality management system [QMS] or another set of requirements).
  - Evaluate capability to perform specific process.
  - Grant approval or preferred supplier status.
  - Award a contract.
  - Surveillance to monitor continued conformance to defined requirements.

- Third-party audit (certification, accreditation, or compliance audits):
  - Assess conformance to identified standard and recommend certification or accreditation.
  - Assess compliance to regulatory requirements.

Based on the audit objectives remote auditing may not be feasible. For example, an initial assessment for certification to ISO 9001 could not be achieved 100 percent remotely due to the need to assess processes and the environment in which they are carried out. However, the stage 1 portion of the audit might under some circumstances be handled remotely. The risk is low because much of the stage 1 assessment involves reviewing documentation to determine if the QMS has been appropriately established and that core processes such as management review and internal auditing have been implemented. Protocols for when to conduct remote audits will also be driven by certification body and accreditation body directives that may limit the options.

For internal audits of a multi-site organization, it might be determined that 50 percent of the processes may be conducted remotely, and the others will be done on site. But, as previously noted, there is value in a remote audit that would allow the auditor to get a customer's perspective of a process such as online quoting to see if there are any problems or risks.

When it comes to supplier audits, the determining factors will be how many of the processes lend themselves to remote auditing and the degree of sophistication of the supplier's technology and electronic infrastructure.

In all instances, the conclusion to be drawn from assessment of this risk is that under current conditions, it would be either difficult or impossible to achieve the outcome that is desired unless factors that contribute to the risks can be effectively addressed. Otherwise, the audit would be ineffective in providing substantive evidence to recommend certification or approve a new supplier or identify problems or close out a corrective action. An ancillary risk would, therefore, be that all the resources expended to conduct the audit would be lost. The audit would have been a useless waste of time.

## Limited random sampling

Sampling is a hallmark of auditing. Although sample plans are primarily associated with inspection and test activities, they do have relevance for the audit process. Generally, the sampling methods are much less formal and not tied to any documented sampling plan. They do, however, share the same goal of determining conformance based on an assessment of a sampling that is reliably representative of the whole.

Guidance for sampling during audits has always relied on considerations such as criticality of a process, variety of evidence supporting the outcome of a process, and the quantity of evidence that is available. For example, a certificate of analysis for stainless steel usually has greater consequence than a certificate of conformance for masking tape. A complex device might have multiple tests that are performed relating to material hardness, fastener torque values, performance under pressure, etc. Whereas another product could undergo a simple pass/fail visual check. For a service provider the product delivered to the customer could be one elaborate installation or hundreds of parcel deliveries. And, one company could fabricate three complete products per month, while another manufactures tens of thousands.

The risk when auditing a process remotely is that the auditor will have underestimated the significance of a category of evidence and requested an inadequate sample size. Or, the sample pulled might not be adequate or representative of the process under normal conditions. In this case, the auditee has included a sample that is an aberration. It's not terribly uncommon. The samples pulled would, for example, reflect one for a demo that a sales representative requested or a training record for an intern program that has been abandoned. When the audit is conducted on-site, it's easy to request additional samples. However, in a remote scenario, the extra evidence might not be easily retrievable. In some instances, it can be retrieved, but not without interruption or delay.

The auditee might have misunderstood the request. Or, at the last minute, someone realized that the sample pulled included proprietary information that can't be transmitted to an unauthorized email address. So, taking all of this into account, the risk is that the sample sizes are inappropriate, not large enough, or adequately homogeneous to make a credible conclusion as to the effectiveness of the process.

## Auditees intimidated by the remote process

The audit process is already fraught with anxiety. Regardless of whether it's an internal audit, an audit conducted by a customer, or an ISO certification assessment, individuals are often loathe to interact with auditors. They feel as though they are being interrogated—that the auditor is looking to trip them up. They fear becoming the obstacle to their organization's ISO certification or the stumbling block to a big contract. It doesn't matter what kind of audit is being conducted. Persons being interviewed find themselves in an unnatural conversation, being asked to explain their jobs and justify decisions that they have made.

This feeling of unease is magnified when the interviewer is a disembodied voice. The onus is upon the auditor to alleviate the tension that might result in auditees being reluctant to respond. A process owner's reticence to respond might be due to a concern about confidentiality or a heightened feeling that they've only got one shot to say the right thing or make the right impression. They don't have their usual props to help them explain. They're not in control of the interview, which leads to a sense of vulnerability.

The obvious risk is that responses will be incomplete and skewed by a sense of intimidation. Later chapters will discuss training and interviewing techniques that can mitigate this risk.

## Inability to perceive the environment in which processes are being conducted

This risk is highly dependent on the nature of the business—the context of the organization. For many organizations, the environment is not particularly relevant to the effectiveness of the process. There are others in which environment has enormous, even dire, consequence for either critical processes or the final product.

Probably the best example would be a clean room setting. It would be essential for the auditor to be able to observe consistent adherence to gowning protocols, environmental controls, and material transfer procedures. This is in addition to the control of the actual processes being conducted. Without access to (and, indeed, agility with) video equipment, tablets, or other monitoring and recording equipment, it would be all but impossible to confidently assess if precautions are effective in preventing damage or contamination of the product.

Examples in other settings could relate to clutter, noise or other distractions, lighting, adequate space, electro-static discharge (ESD) precautions, weather, security, or control of environmentally sensitive material.

## Maintaining integrity of process

It's important to bear in mind what has been previously discussed about the definition of remote auditing. It's appropriate to reiterate that this is not a new kind of audit. Auditors are simply employing different tools and methods to achieve the audit objective. The same fundamentals relating to objectivity, confidentiality, evidence-based decisions, and risk-based approach are still applicable. Auditors must apply the same rigor as they would to an on-site audit.

Let's use the case of an organization with multiple sites that has decided to split its internal audit program, performing half of the audits on-site and the balance remotely. If during the course of the remote audit it became apparent that some evidence was simply unavailable or that the samples that had been pulled were not adequately representative of the process, it would not be acceptable to say: "We'll just go with what we've got and catch it up next year." If the audit did not allow for the assessment of adequate pertinent information, appropriate sampling, or access to responsible process owners, the audit has not achieved its objective. If the auditor can't perceive the inputs, activities, and outputs, the audit is, at best, incomplete and should be repeated. Consideration of the risks during the planning activities along with some training should mitigate those instances when the audit is unsuccessful.

Examples of other activities that would impinge on the integrity of the audit process might include auditees pulling samples that are not adequately randomized, individuals providing digital images of processes selecting only those operating under pristine conditions, angling of video devices to frame most desirable shots of a work environment, and choosing what personnel may be available for interview. Although the examples could appear to be deliberately calculating or misleading, in many instances it's either innocent happenstance or just the normal human tendency to cast oneself in the most favorable light. Nobody wants to look bad or make their boss look bad. Other times, neither the auditor nor the auditee has given adequate thought ahead of the audit and the evidence presented just isn't sufficient or appropriate.

This is less likely to occur during an on-site audit. The auditor can ask for additional samples of a test report or request to see another production cell operating or rearrange the schedule for when the process owner is available.

As previously mentioned, planning and training will mitigate some of this. Included in that planning should be a discussion with the auditee about issues such as sample sizes and the availability of staff.

The degree to which this particular risk can be managed is reliant on the next two identified risks.

## Limitations of technology

This risk must be managed for a remote audit to proceed. The levels of complexity and prevalence of advanced technology across the various organizational functions varies markedly in industries. And, they aren't particularly reliant on size or product. There are small machine shops that have been driven to implement advanced communications methods by their customer base. A large customer may mandate that quotations, orders, and all issues be handled through their web-based portal. At the other end of the spectrum are larger companies so impeded by the inertia of their enormous and complex electronic infrastructure that upgrading to more sophisticated equipment is a Herculean undertaking. They may still have systems operating on outdated or legacy software that isn't well integrated into web-based platforms. The point is auditors can't assume a certain level of technological sophistication.

So, what kind of questions need to be answered before embarking on the audit?

- What web conferencing platform, if any, do they have?
- What ERP system is used?
- Does their web conferencing platform accommodate screen sharing?
- Do they have basic teleconferencing equipment?

- Is their document control cloud-based?
- Does the organization use hand-held scanning guns, tablets, or smart phones?
- Can they transfer documents to PDF format for emailing?
- Do the key players, both auditors and auditees, know how to use this stuff?
- Are any of their processes reliant on artificial intelligence?

Answers to these questions will drive that portion of the planning process related to communication, access to data, interviewing, and observing of processes. It will determine if some processes can be audited remotely while others need to be observed on site. It will also determine the kind of training auditors may need.

## Security and confidentiality concerns

This last risk is somewhat related to the discussion about technology. The type of technology used should drive security protocols. Those protocols will determine feasibility as well as required authorizations and protocols to be followed.

It may be that access can be granted; however, special conditions in addition to the standard nondisclosure agreement will be required. There may be a request from the auditee to validate the security of the auditor's system. There may be cases in which the auditee is contractually prohibited from electronic sharing of certain documents or information. For audits involving international organizations it's also important to verify compliance with laws and agreements such as the General Data Protection Regulation (GDPR) in the European Union.

In most instances, all that is required is either written or verbal acceptance of the company's security protocols. Remember that any files that have been downloaded need to be protected. Any video clips on cell phones need to be deleted. Sometimes the auditee requires that the electronic files be completely deleted from the auditor's system upon completion of the audit. In other cases, the onus is on the auditor to decide what to keep and how to protect it.

As a side note, management system experts often think of opportunity as the other side of the risk-based thinking coin. In this case, the unique benefit presented by this particular risk is that it allows the auditor to assess the integrity of the auditee's system for protecting its documented information— which is a requirement of most management system standards.

## Putting It All Together

It's a good idea to develop a checklist of these risk categories with some adjustment for the industry in which you work and the kinds of audits to be conducted. Vetting of these issues will facilitate both the planning and effective implementation of the audit program.

Finally, it bears repeating that there are some instances in which the result of the risk assessment will yield the conclusion that a remote audit cannot be effectively conducted. The existing constraints are too significant to expect that the audit objective could be achieved. In those instances, the decision must be to proceed with an on-site audit with appropriate planning to mitigate any other identified risks.

# CHAPTER 4

# Planning the Remote Audit

E ffective planning is one of the hallmarks of a successful audit program. As with any process or project the planning that precedes deployment is a dependable indicator of the reliability of the output.

Regardless if the program deals with internal audits, supplier audits, or certification assessments there are common factors to consider. The audit plan must consider various constraints, including the size and layout of the facility, number of sites, time zones, individual schedules, and the general availability of process owners. Consideration of the risks that have been previously identified facilitates developing audit plans that produce the most informative results.

## Creating an Annual Schedule

An annual schedule should be established. For an internal audit program this will include all processes within the scope of the management system, audited at determined locations and defined frequencies. There will probably be a variation in frequency that is consistent with guidance found in ISO 9001 and comparable management system standards relative to the importance of processes and changes that could affect the management system. Examples that would warrant greater frequency might include a design process that is driven by customer requirements or a manufacturing area that has a high turnover of personnel. Conversely, there may be a process that had previously been plagued by problems that drove the need for more frequent monitoring through internal audits. However, it has now become a model of control and efficiency. The organization might decide to decrease the frequency of audits of that function from quarterly to only twice per year.

During the development of the schedule the manager of the audit program would determine the appropriate frequencies for each audit. With a multi-site facility, there could be two locations that ship product. However, one of them only ships replacement components that are warehoused in sealed containers, while the other ships out complete assemblies. It could be determined that one site could be audited remotely, while the other would undergo the traditional on-site audit. Other examples could include the manufacturing site doing a remote audit of the management review process that is carried out at the main facility or auditors at the warehouse location doing a remote audit of the online quotation process using a perspective not unlike the one experienced by customers.

The schedule that is developed could be a temporary departure from a standard plan due to constraints such as that created by the 2020 COVID-19 pandemic. Or, it could be a decision based upon an assessment of feasibility and benefits that has led to the conclusion that remote audits should be an integral component of the entire program.

Figure 4.1 on page 19 presents an annual audit schedule for an organization that has facilities in three cities within the same region. One plant conducts all processes; the other two are a secondary manufacturing site and a warehousing facility.

A similar method seen in figure 4.2 on page 20 can be employed for supplier audits. In this example, critical suppliers are audited twice per year. Although there are some instances in which the audits are still conducted on-site, there are others where the determination has been made that at least one of the audits can occur remotely.

Because about half of the suppliers are in Europe or in the Asia-Pacific region, there is a considerable time and money savings to be achieved. The decision is partially driven by answers to questions about technology and access. So, while it's important to start with the schedule, conversations with suppliers will probably result in some adjustments to the plan.

## Figure 4.1: Annual internal audit schedule

| | | Plant 1 | | | | Plant 2 | | | Warehouse | |
|---|---|---|---|---|---|---|---|---|---|---|
| | | Jan | Jul | Apr | Nov | Feb | Aug | Nov | Mar | Sep |
| Audit Type* | | OS | R | OS | R | OS | R | OS | OS | R |
| | Purchasing | X | | | X | | | | | |
| | Receiving | X | | | | | | | X | |
| | Production | X | | X | | X | X | | | |
| | Inspection and Test | X | | X | | X | X | | X | |
| | Shipping | X | | | | | | | | |
| | Control of NC Material | X | | X | | X | | | X | |
| | Preventive Maintenance | | X | X | | | X | X | | X |
| | Engineering | X | X | | X | | X | | | |
| | Document Control | X | X | | X | | X | X | | X |
| Processes/Activity | Training | | X | X | | | X | | | X |
| | Calibration | X | X | | X | X | X | X | X | |
| | Design | X | | X | | | | | | |
| | Corrective Actions | | X | | X | | | | | X |
| | Warehousing & Traceability | X | | | | X | | | X | |
| | Scheduling | | X | | X | | X | | | X |
| | Quoting | X | | | X | | | | | |
| | Order Entry | X | | | X | X | | | | |
| | Internal Audits | | X | | | | | | | |
| | Management Review | | X | | | | | | | |

*OS = On-Site Audit/R = Remote Audit.

## Figure 4.2: Supplier audit schedule (new and existing)

| | | Jan | Feb | Mar | Apr | May | June | Aug | Sept | Oct |
|---|---|---|---|---|---|---|---|---|---|---|
| **Audit Type*** | | OS | R | OS | R | OS | R | OS | OS | R |
| | Ajax Castings | X | | | | X | | | | |
| | Design Assoc. | X | | | | | X | | | |
| | Pure Steel Co. | | | X | | | | | X | |
| | McClean Gaskets | | | | | X | | | X | |
| | Electronics First Co. | | X | | | | | X | | |
| Supplier | Board Assembly Inc. | | | X | | | | X | | |
| | Microvalves Inc. | X | | | X | | | | | |
| | Desmond Inc. | | | X | | | X | | | |
| | Brandy and Cooper Co. | | | | | X | | | | X |
| | Prisms Corp. | | X | | | | | X | | |
| | Fasteners Distribution | | X | | | | X | | | |
| | Reserved for New Suppliers | X | | X | | X | | X | | X |

*OS = On-Site Audit/R = Remote Audit.

## Time zones

While putting the program together, there will need to be consideration of the time zone in which the auditees operate. This can be relevant for first-, second-, and third-party audits. Practically speaking, it's probably most applicable to supplier audits. They're the ones that are most likely to be on another continent.

As you plan the remote audits, you'll need to arrive at a time slot that works for both parties. Occasionally, you'll find suppliers who operate three shifts or who have decided to make relevant personnel available whenever the customer wants. That's very accommodating. But what happens if you need to interview five or six people? Are they all going to be able to be on a call at 11:00 p.m.?

If you're dealing with internal audits, you probably already know the timing constraints, but it's a good idea to verify them ahead of time.

## Available Technology

This information should be discussed during the same conversation about time zones. Again, this is usually more relevant when dealing with suppliers. For internal audits, it may not be whether the technology exists. It may simply be: What is the level of agility with the software and equipment among the individuals you'll need to interview?

The typical equipment and software you'll be dealing with includes:

- Tablets and smart phones
- Web conferencing platforms
- Screen sharing
- Teleconferencing
- Email access and security
- Drones

It's important to plan a time prior to the audit to test out the equipment. Considerations include:

- Does the web conferencing software require you to send an invite?
- Does the auditee have to download software in advance?
- Does the supplier have a firewall?
- Will screen sharing be available for all processes or just some of them?
- How stable are internet connections?
- Does the auditee need a web camera? If so, is it portable?
- Will those being interviewed come to a conference room or will multiple cameras be used?
- Do certain areas need to be accessible to the camera?
- Does the microphone on the teleconferencing gizmo work?

- What happens if the call gets dropped or the platform terminates a web session?

Asking these questions and testing the system will mitigate telecommunication meltdowns that could doom the audit.

The other hedge against a meltdown is a backup plan. Consider in advance what you will do if the equipment fails or individuals experience problems with using some unfamiliar tools like web conferencing. This will prevent loss of time and the potential of having to reschedule the audit—and starting all over again.

For example, you may have planned for the auditee to use screen-sharing technology. The internet connection is too slow and keeps timing out. Having planned for this potential eventuality, you say: "OK. Let's try this another way. Could you please capture screen shots of the process at these four defined points? Please email them to me along with copies of the job order and final assembly drawing. We'll use a regular phone line for the interview. I'll call you back in 45 minutes."

This demonstration of professionalism should ease the auditee's stress over the perceived failure and allows the audit to proceed.

One final note on use of technology: Some organizations are not going to have anything beyond rudimentary tools like a phone line and emailing capabilities. If that's all they have got, that's what you will have to work with. The process will not be as streamlined, but the audit objective is still achievable.

## Training and Competence

The assumption is that you already have trained auditors. Although they will have achieved the requisite level of competence as auditors, they may not be able to demonstrate competence in the skills and method needed to successfully conduct audits remotely. This is probably not a good time to bring on a new auditor.

Most of what is thrown into the general category of training will in many instances be either refresher training or informational discussions on specifically targeted topics. You'll want to provide additional training on the areas listed below.

## Use of various technology, as appropriate

This goes beyond simple familiarity. The goal here is to ensure actual hands-on experience. Skyping with the grandkids is not the same as coordinating an interview with individuals in three different states that includes screensharing. For video conferencing that involves panning out to display a work area, it's best to have had some rudimentary practice prior to going live. To that end, for this category of training, a trial run or simulated scenario might be the best way to go.

## Tips for remote interviewing

Teleconferencing presents challenges that are unique when it comes to the interviewing process. Etiquette is one of the subsets of auditor principles. It relates to conducting oneself with integrity and professional ethics. When you're dealing with teleconferencing there is no video image to observe. So, there needs to be a heightened deliberate consciousness of the way auditors behave in a remote environment.

Expect to have to speak more slowly and clearly.

In the absence of visual cues, it is especially important to be sensitive to the tempo of the conversation. When interviewing face-to-face it's easy to see if someone isn't speaking because they're gathering their thoughts to give you the best answer. In a teleconference, all you have is dead air. Even with video conferencing, the lack of proximity seems to make conversations more stilted and inhibiting.

It's useful to remind auditors of this divergence from the typical interviewing experience. It's a good idea to have follow-up questions prepared to use after a brief silence. Another tack would be to rephrase the question, referring to documents and records that have previously been furnished.

In the next chapter, prepping for each individual audit will be discussed. One of the activities involves the review of documented procedures and any evidence that has been furnished prior to the interview. This facilitates the interviewing process. It is also another application of the rules of etiquette, in that the auditor logs on or calls in well prepared. No one's time is wasted with distracting paper shuffles or with the annoying clicking through screens trying to get to the right piece of evidence.

## Sample size

It's important to remind the auditors of the downfall of inadequate planning when it comes to sample selection. The best tactic to ensure sufficient and appropriate samples is to gain understanding of the process through review of documents, work instructions, manuals, and procedures.

Sample sizes will vary from one audit to the next, depending on the scope of the audit and complexity of processes. More information is found in the next chapter on prepping for each audit.

## Security and confidentiality

Auditors should be well briefed on security protocols. If they are conducting audits using their own personal laptops or phones, it's essential to remind them of some of these potential pitfalls:

- Consequences of not confirming permission to access and view company documents
- Inadvertent disclosure of supplier, client, or company information through a breached or porous firewall
- Breach of contract for failing to delete downloaded files at the end of the audit
- Risk of viral infection by not ensuring security of the auditee's internet connection

These are the fundamental factors that go into planning an efficient program for remote audits. When initially setting up an audit program, make sure to include adequate time for thoughtful planning. Like so many other things, this small investment can pay big dividends. Develop good plans and use them.

# CHAPTER FIVE

# Prepping for a Remote Audit

P reparations for individual audits are more detailed than audit program plans. They involve determination of the activities that will be audited, the documents to be reviewed, the samples to be requested, and the individuals who will be interviewed. The prep work can vary considerably from one audit to the next.

Let's take the example of an organization that has decided to do a surveillance audit of a previously qualified supplier's production processes. The scope of activities will be planning, material traceability, all machining operations, in-process inspections and tests, final inspection, and release for shipping.

Prior to the audit, it will be necessary to gain access to the documented information that defines the control of these processes. Because "documented procedures" are not always a requirement of management system standards, this might be a bit challenging. This, along with other logistical considerations, can best be handled through a phone call but can sometimes be managed through email communication. The point is the need for communication. Getting hold of these documents comes first.

Note that as soon as the documentation has been received, the audit process begins. Auditing requires verification of evidence that a process has been:

- Sufficiently determined and defined.
- Implemented under controlled conditions that are consistent with that which was determined.
- Effective in achieving desired outcomes.

Reviewing the documented information in whatever format it is presented is the first step toward accomplishing this verification. So, although you haven't conducted an opening meeting or started interviewing staff, the audit is underway. This review allows the auditor to assess the adequacy of the way the requirements have been determined and defined. "Document procedures" may not be a requirement. However, there is a requirement that inputs are determined, defined, and accessible to individuals who need them in a format that is appropriate to the function.

Assessment of the documents should facilitate adequate understanding of the processes to begin building the audit plan in earnest. In this scenario, we'll posit that the documented information describing processes and their interrelations is contained at a high level in their quality manual—not a whole bunch of detail. Afterward, all instructions and customer requirements are embedded into production routers that are unique to each customer part number. The routers are partially derived from the estimating module within the ERP system. The only other documents are work instructions for the sampling plan and the checklist for product release. This preliminary information is garnered from a conversation (or email) with the company contact.

To put the plan together you need the quality manual, the sampling plan, a blank product release checklist, and one example of a completed router. If this is a surveillance audit, it's possible that you already have copies of some of these documents. Then again, if there are high levels of security, you may have been required to destroy any evidence that had been acquired during the initial qualification audit.

Once you've had a chance to review this set of documents, you should have adequate information to put the plan together. Just as with an on-site audit, you need to establish times for various interviews and a sequence that will allow for the most effective and efficient assessment of the processes.

During the earlier planning process, the manager of your company's supplier audit program will have acquired information about web conferencing capabilities and any other technology that will facilitate the audit. In this instance, you have learned that they can use an app on their tablets to display manufacturing areas in real time. They also have web conferencing software that will allow screen sharing which they supplement with a phone line for teleconferencing.

You put together your plan. Time slots are assigned with breaks in between to handle logistics and to check in with your contact in case you need more samples. Remember to be sensitive to break times and avoid the lunch hour.

The plan includes identification of the individuals that you will want to interview. This identification is by function—not by name. You'll want to speak to the scheduler. During that interview, you expect that he or she will be able to share his or her screen so that you can observe how scheduling is accomplished in the ERP system. Afterward, you'd like to interview four machine operators and get a screen pan of their work areas that will give you the ability to see the operation, the measuring equipment they use for in-process inspections, and the production routers and drawings on their workbench. Then you'll want to interview the quality technician who does final inspection and the quality control manager who does the final product release.

Inform your contact that you'll need to see the following samples of evidence prior to beginning the interviews: five completed routers, five final inspection reports, and three completed final release checklists. Then you finalize the schedule for the audit.

You allocate:
- 10 minutes for an opening meeting
- 20 minutes for each interview
- 5 minutes between each interview
- One 20-minute break for both you and the company contact person
- 15 minutes for recap of all that has been assessed thus far
- 20 minutes to request additional samples or follow-up interviews
- 30 minutes to complete the extra interview(s) and review additional evidence

- 20 minutes to complete the summary (not detailed) audit report
- 20 minutes for a closing meeting, including comments, findings, and/or recommendations

This part of the audit where there is direct interaction with the auditee will take approximately three hours. The total time devoted to the audit (not including prep work and audit report) is closer to six hours because a considerable amount of time will have been consumed with the initial review of documents and records.

This example is obviously not an audit of a complete management system. But it illustrates most of the activities that should precede an audit. In short, you need to:

- Get documentation that allows you to understand processes.
- Determine telecommunication or web conferencing capabilities.
- Know the production work schedule (start time, breaks, lunch, etc.).
- Understand how many unique sub-processes or operations are within the scope of the audit.
- Understand the methodology for product verification.
- Determine types of evidence and sample sizes that you'll require.
- Decide whom to interview and how many people.
- Allocate enough time to conduct the audit successfully.

Of all of these, perhaps the one step that will most facilitate the interview process is the prior acquisition of samples. This enhances your understanding of the process. You can use them to frame the questions you will ask. For example, using the same scenario, we can consider the information that is derived from a review of some completed production routers. You note the following:

- There is a field for recording the heat number for the aluminum used, indicating their method of material traceability.
- The machine settings are in editable format, suggesting that the operators either program each job or have the capability to make adjustment to the equipment set-up.

- There's a quality control sign-off for some operations, meaning some in-process inspections are done by the operators and others require verification by a quality technician.
- There's a column for recording actual run time, providing the raw data used for monitoring job efficiency.

From just these few observations will come the list of questions for the interview with the machine operators and quality control manager. The part numbers, job numbers, and manufacturing instructions provide you with references that are recognizable to the auditees. There will be jargon and acronyms and names that are familiar to them, alleviating the awkwardness of being interviewed by a disembodied voice. It will reassure the auditee that there's a person behind the voice who has some understanding of the work that they do. This eases some of the discomfort and mitigates the risk of an unsuccessful interview.

The final step before you initiate the opening meeting is to create the checklist. This will be based on all the questions that have arisen while reviewing the documentation. Back to the process approach:

- What are the inputs?
- What are the activities?
- What are the outputs?
- What are the support processes?
- What are the contingencies if something goes wrong?
- Is the process conducted and controlled as defined?
- What records are retained?
- Does the process achieve its intended result?

Prepping for an audit demonstrate professionalism. It communicates to auditees that you take this audit seriously. You have bothered to take the time to learn about them. You have an appreciation of their time and respect for their organization.

# Examples of Evidence

Below are typical examples of evidence that may be requested ahead of an audit. In some cases, depending on the scope of the audit, the remote review and assessment of this evidence will occupy a considerable portion of the total audit.

## Management review

Get the records of at least two recent management reviews. This will ensure that you can assess the review of status of actions from previous reviews and changes in performance indicators.

## Performance data

Let the auditee know that you need the performance data that substantiates the management review. You'll also want to see the data used to monitor progress of quality objectives. If they use a dashboard, ask for copies of the last two quarters. Finally, ask if there are any other important metrics that are tracked and analyzed.

## Internal audits

Ask for copies of at least five internal audits. This is a good example of when it's helpful to have reviewed some of their procedures ahead of time. That way, if they only do one massive annual audit, you'll know that asking for more than one report is not going to work. But you also know that if there's only one, it will undergo greater scrutiny. Let's assume they do them monthly. Make sure to let the contact person know, you'd like to see records of internal audits that have been done in the last 8–10 months.

## Corrective actions

Request a total of five corrective actions: two from audit findings and three from customer complaints. Make sure that you ask for completed corrective actions so that you can assess verification of effectiveness of the action taken.

## Purchase orders

To get a holistic sense of the control of the purchasing function, it's a good idea to get samples from various kinds of suppliers. That's not always possible. In some cases, the company only has six vendors that it uses for 95 percent of its production-related purchases. For this scenario, we are assuming more variety. This will also allow you to observe different product acceptance methods for different categories of purchases. Therefore, the request will be for orders that have been received. You would request two from raw material suppliers, one from a customized fabrication house, two for outsourced processes, and two for off-the-shelf components (like valves or gaskets). That leads you to the accompanying request as seen below.

## Receiving/product acceptance records

You'll want to see the receiving records or product acceptance records for each purchase order. This should yield two certificates of analysis for raw materials, two final test reports for outsourced processes, one in-house detailed incoming inspection report, one standard certificate of conformance, and one certificate with the product shelf-life. This shows both the process approach and the systems approach applied to the audit process. The inputs are the purchase orders; the outputs are the receiving records.

## Quotations

You'll want to see five quotations for which customer orders have been received. Ask for samplings that reflect repeat orders, standard parts, and customized (or new design) product. If the company also does servicing installation or repair, add that to the mix.

## Customer orders

This is pretty much like the purchasing example above. Ask for the customer orders. Here's one of the most prominent examples of confidential information. If the auditee emails PDFs of customer orders, you want to ensure the information is protected while you're using it and discarded when you are done. Other examples that often accompany both customer orders and quotations are drawings and other proprietary files in any format.

## Certificates of calibration

This last example is a bit of an outlier. Generally, during an on-site audit, we look at the instruments in use and then backtrack into the records of calibration. But, having at least two or three certificates ahead of time starts the conversation. This is one that is reliant on getting either video or photos of tools on the floor—complete with visible calibration stickers.

It should be apparent from looking at the list of evidence that there will be a lot of times when additional samples—or different samples—will have to be requested. Starting with a smaller and less specified sampling increases the likelihood that more samples will be needed. Hence adding that contingency time into the schedule.

The finalized schedule has now been sent to the contact person at the auditee's location. Encourage that individual to share the schedule with all persons who will be involved in the audit. Reiterate the start time and request that people sign in early to make sure all the bugs have been worked out of the technology and equipment you'll be using.

Having digested all the information and confirmed everything with the auditee, it's time to begin the opening meeting and the interviews.

# CHAPTER SIX

# Conducting the Remote Audit

You've completed all of your preparations. The documents have been reviewed; the schedule has been circulated to key players. It's time to log-on or call in.

Even if you've planned for an audio-only web call, be prepared for the annoying possibility that the webcam on your laptop will activate. This is a business meeting and your appearance should reflect appropriate professionalism. Try to call in a few minutes before the scheduled start time in anticipation of any glitches. Confirm that all participants are on the call and that the equipment is working properly. Remind people to mute their phones. Suggest closing doors or using other means to diminish noise, distractions, or interruptions.

## The Opening Meeting

All audits have an opening meeting. Depending on the type of audits, they vary in length and complexity. Certification bodies tend to have extensive lists of items that must be covered during an opening meeting. Even with less prescriptive formats, there are some common elements that should be covered including:

- Introductions
- Scope of the audit

- Audit objective
- Confidentiality and security
- Description of audit method
- Explanation of possible findings
- Review of the audit schedule

Most of these are straightforward. However, due to the lack of familiarity with the methods used in remote auditing, they may require either elaboration or inclusion of additional considerations. What follows are those aspects of a remote auditing opening meeting that require a little extra discussion.

## Introductions

Introductions for remote auditing require focus on who is in attendance. For a face-to-face meeting, it's easy to see who is in the room and who is speaking. For teleconferencing, there are no visual cues. Even with web-conferencing, there are times when all participants can't be viewed due to the positioning of the webcam. So, getting a handle on who's in the virtual meeting takes a little more finesse.

Speak slowly and clearly. If you didn't hear someone's name or title, ask the person to repeat. Be patient. And, remember that the tension or annoyance in your voice is often magnified because they don't have your physical presence to distract them. The need for vigilant attention to clear and measured speech holds true throughout the entire audit.

## Scope of the audit

The scope of the audit would not vary from what you'd state during a face-to-face opening meeting. ISO 19011 defines audit scope as "...extent and boundaries of an audit." These boundaries could refer to specific processes, locations, manufacturing shifts, or product lines. During a third-party surveillance audit, the scope might be the core quality management system (QMS) processes (such as management review, internal auditing, risk, and corrective action) plus purchasing, receiving, manufacturing, inspection, and packaging of product for the main manufacturing plant. For a supplier periodic surveillance, it could be an audit of the outsourced process that the company provides. Essentially, the scope defines what is within and (by default) what is outside of the boundaries of a particular visit.

## Audit objective

The audit objective was discussed in chapter three. To recap, it relates to what you wish to achieve. A brief reiteration of the most common examples of audit objectives:

- First-party audit (internal audits):
  - Determine conformance to management systems requirements such as ISO 9001.
  - Identify problems and risks.

- Second-party audit (supplier audits):
  - Evaluate capability to perform specific process.
  - Grant approval or preferred supplier status.
  - Award a contract.

- Third-party audit (certification, accreditation, or compliance audits):
  - Assess conformance to identified standard and recommend certification.
  - Assess compliance to regulatory requirements.

## Confidentiality and security

Confidentiality earns extra time during the opening meeting due to the level of risk and the anxiety it can create. The auditor should reassure all participants that security concerns have been addressed during the planning process. There should be a clear description of what measures are being employed to protect information. It's generally the case that the auditor invites questions just prior to the conclusion of the opening. However, confidentiality and security are of such critical concern to many people that it's best to get the questions answered as soon as they arise.

## Description of audit method

This is the item on the opening meeting agenda that will be the greatest divergence from a face-to-face event. It's paramount that everyone understands that this is a real and legitimate audit, carrying the same weight as "regular" audits they've experienced in the past. There are the same requirements for interviewing, reviewing of documents, and gathering of evidence. "It's just that we are doing things differently." What ensues is your explanation of the following:

- Why remote auditing method is being utilized
- What documents and evidence have already been reviewed
- How the audit schedule was developed
- What technology will be utilized
- How the interviews will be conducted
- What will happen after the audit is concluded

This is a narrative. It is not a discussion or an open forum. Ask people to hold their questions until after the audit schedule has been reviewed.

## Explanation of possible audit findings

This is a fundamental element of any audit. The findings do not change. Although there are shades of difference between internal audits, supplier qualifications, certification assessment, and regulatory audits they usually boil down to the following three:

- *Major nonconformance*—a complete breakdown of process or system.
- *Minor nonconformance*—the nonfulfillment of a requirement.
- *Observation*—an opportunity for improvement or a perception of risk.

Consistent with the rules of auditing, it is appropriate for the auditee to be notified in advance of the classification method for potential findings.

## Review of the audit schedule

The schedule should have been previously circulated to key participants. And, the contact person should have also solicited their questions or concerns so that they could be addressed. This may have already happened prior to the opening meeting and been handled through a series of emails. Despite those precautions, there may still be some last-minute conflicts or other problems. Work them out as best you can without compromising the integrity of your audit.

After the schedule has finally been vetted, invite additional questions. Respond completely and efficiently. You need to conclude the opening meeting so that the audit may begin.

# Off-Site Document Review

The audit began when you started reviewing the virtual mounds of documented information that hit your inbox. In some instances, the items reviewed will serve to tee up interviews. But there are other documents and records whose off-site review will constitute most if not all the assessment of a process. Internal audits and management review are two good examples. In each case the information is all laid out. Interviewing will often be brief. That doesn't mean there aren't great questions to be asked. Management review is frequently audited off-site during Stage 1 assessments. The questions that arise relate to decisions made based on risk assessment, actions taken on negatively trending process performance, initiatives launched based on market feedback, incorporation of strategic planning into the quality management system, etc. The responses will allow the auditor to assess top management commitment and the effectiveness of its review process.

So, you come to the first interview with a lot of knowledge, some questions, and a need for many more answers.

---

# Interviewing

After the opening meeting is concluded, it's time to bring in the first auditee. You are logged in to the web-conferencing program that accommodates screen sharing. Your contact person will be responsible for coordinating individuals' arrival into the designated meeting room and for making required adjustments to equipment. Remind individuals that their microphones are live even when there's a brief interruption to the interview.

In this example the purchasing manager has password protected access to the ERP system. During the interview, he or she will transit through all the screens and modules used to run monthly demand reports, access history, and inventory turns data; check for recent supplier quotations; and verify current lead time for parts. Then he or she will demonstrate how an order is generated and how it is automatically emailed to the supplier, with drawings and other attachments if required. Along the way, the auditor interjects questions based upon what is being described and any documentation that has been previously reviewed.

When that interview is completed the design engineer enters the meeting room. He or she has his or her own engineering server with software that is again password protected. Therefore, a few minutes of transition should be allocated between the two interviews to allow for closing and logging out of one function's files and re-booting to access a different server for another function. Then, again via the web conferencing link, screen sharing allows for viewing documents and programs. This provides two things: an ability to gather evidence about the unique process that is the subject of the interview and an opportunity to assess the competence of individuals and the integrity of their documentation control system.

Other times the communication will utilize less sophisticated technology. The only equipment is the telephone. All evidence has been furnished previously via email. The auditor asks questions about how the process is implemented, using the evidence to frame the questions. It's important that the auditees are aware of the exact samples that have been furnished for your review. This provides them the opportunity to either bring copies of the evidence to the meeting room or to have refreshed their memory of the information prior to the interview.

It's essential to be clear about what evidence is being cited when conducting the interview. The auditor does not have the luxury of simply pointing and saying, "What does that mean?" A question might be: "I noticed that on purchase orders 7834 and 7901 that the revision level is clearly indicated. However, for purchase orders 7895 and 7899, there is no revision level noted—even though the supplier quotation VS3325 does include the drawing revision number. What is the difference?" The point is that, in the absence of readily available props (i.e., physical evidence), the auditor must be clear about what documented information is being referenced.

When video conferencing, there may be some visual cues to perceive if an auditee is confused or frustrated. It's a little easier to read the body language. If you're just using the telephone, the visual cues are gone and when the auditee is having trouble understanding the question, all you have is dead air. When the awkward silence occurs, it's the auditor's job to either restate the question or explain the requirement in such a way that the auditee understands what evidence is required to prove conformance.

Be prepared to explain your question, using the procedures and evidence to frame what you are trying to verify. Be clear without sounding pedantic. Be gracious and patient, but persistent. Basically, regardless of the audit format, the goal is still the same. The requirements (inputs) are spelled out; the evidence (output) is presented. Do they match?

Somewhere in the middle of any one of these interviews it may become apparent that you need more samples of evidence. There are a variety of reasons that are no one's fault. You didn't fully understand a process. There's an extra step that isn't well documented. The contact person misinterpreted your request. The sample size isn't representative of the normal process. The samples provided have raised additional questions.

Here's when the contingency time you built into the audit schedule pays off. You inform the auditee that you need the samples. It will take 20 minutes to retrieve them because the person who handles the records just went on break. You decide we can all use a break. The decision is made to hang up and to resume in 30 minutes. Be sure everyone agrees on:

- The time to call back in
- The exact evidence that is expected when you reconvene
- Whether to leave the web conferencing portion of the call open or close it out and re-boot
- If anyone needs to be notified because this may affect the rest of the schedule

When everyone returns you do need to do a brief check to make sure the equipment is still functioning properly. You repeat the process for several interviewees.

Conducting several interviews back-to-back can be tedious. There are several aspects of the process that aren't normal. Auditors are required to be observant and perceptive with an ability to grasp the holistic nature of an organization—the interdependencies and interrelations of processes. The need for heightened vigilance to compensate for the lack of visual cues, ease of access to ancillary functions, and the lack of proximity eventually create stress. Remote audits are no easier.

Representatives of top management are generally interviewed in relation to the management review process, planning, and their overall engagement in the management system. If the remote audit has been the result of an unforeseen event such as the COVID-19 pandemic, it's appropriate to ask questions about the identified risks, how they are being addressed, and plans for returning to normal operation.

At some point you may need to move out of the stable environment of a meeting room. The best example is when you need to audit the manufacturing processes. As mentioned previously, this portion of the audit is dependent on the integrity and veracity of the auditee. The auditor is depending on the individuals at the remote location to point their cameras, smart phones, or tablets in such a way as to allow the process to be observed objectively and holistically. The auditee should be able to pan through the working cell pausing at the direction of the auditor to allow viewing of machine settings, raw material lot numbers, in-process inspection records, drawings, calibration stickers, and finished parts. There should be an opportunity for the auditor to ask several questions and for the machine operator to respond using the evidence at hand to demonstrate the process.

Take copious notes. Unlike an on-site audit, there is rarely a chance to go back and grab that work order number you missed or the revision level on the drawing in the quality control lab. Be thorough the first time because the opportunity for follow-up is limited.

There must be adequate and well-documented evidence to compensate for the lack of direct face-to-face interaction with the auditee and the inability to fully assess the actual environment. The evidence substantiates the audit conclusion. Without the touching, seeing, smelling of an on-site audit the documents and records take on a weightier portion of the audit report and the subsequent conclusion. Good notes will get you there.

If this is the organization's first experience with remote auditing, reiterate the fact that you are aware that this is unusual and may be unsettling. At the end of each interview, re-confirm the commitment to confidentiality and information security. For functions like contract review or design explain the protocols for protecting and/or destroying any proprietary information that has been acquired during the audit. Advise the auditee of any findings.

And, make sure you say thanks.

## The Closing Meeting

Once all the interviews are complete, request time to put together a summary report. You'll want to log-off the call. Determine a time to reconvene. Put together your notes for the closing meeting. These will include:

- Reiteration of scope and audit objective
- Assurance that confidential information will be disposed of in accordance with agreement
- Brief summary of what was observed
- Findings of nonconformity and opportunities for improvement
- Requests for corrective action, as needed

- Possible anticipated follow-up actions
- Recommendations, as appropriate

Conduct the closing meeting as you would on-site with the small adaptions as previously noted for the opening meeting. Ensure that individuals in attendance understand any findings that have been raised. Inform the auditee when the full report will be sent and discuss timeline for response to any corrective actions or other follow-up.

If the remote audit has been a new experience for either the auditor or the auditee, solicit feedback. This will be valuable information for future planning.

Thank the participants, conclude the meeting, and get ready to write your report.

# CHAPTER 7

# Writing the Audit Report

Most of the audit report will mirror others that have been written. If it's an internal audit, the report may be incorporated into the checklist. There may be separate forms for audit findings. For supplier reports, there'll be more elaboration of processes that are of particular interest to the organization (for example, a process that the company will outsource to the successful candidate). In addition, there may be an action plan to help the company better comply with your organization's requirements or there could be a recommendation for approval. The rules of audit reporting for remote certification audits are governed by certification bodies.

## What to Include in the Audit Report

Audit reports should contain the following information:
- Date of the audit
- Scope of the audit (areas and functions audited)
- Standard used (e.g., ISO 9001, FAA regulations, or the company's own procedures)
- Name of the lead auditor
- The people interviewed (either by name or by function/title)
- Summary of what was observed

- Benchmarks and opportunities for improvement
- Findings

---

# Remote Audit Report Additions

For remote audits there are a few details that need to be added or elaborated upon.

The summary should describe how the audit was conducted. The auditor should provide the reason for the remote nature of the audit, the technology that was used, how the audit proceeded, and what, if any, constraints inhibited the flow of the audit. There should be a reiteration of the confidentiality and security protocols established. This summary should be detailed.

The rationale for conducting the audit utilizing remote techniques should be clear. There should be reference made to identified risks (such as those presented by the COVID-19 pandemic). Other rationales might include the need to qualify a supplier quickly to coordinate with the manufacturing timeline for a new product release. Or, the auditor with the requisite technical expertise has limited time and couldn't travel to the other side of the globe.

The information and communications technology (ICT) that was used should be described. For example:

> *Skype was used with screen sharing of the ERP system and the engineering files. Two individuals joined the meeting by telephone. A video cam was used to interview individuals in manufacturing and the quality control lab.*

This gives the audit client (person or organization who requested the audit) a clear picture of the conditions under which the audit was conducted. The information should be sufficiently detailed to give confidence that the results of the audit are reliable. This is a good spot in the summary to insert a brief statement of agreed upon arrangements for protection and disposal of confidential files that will have been downloaded during the audit.

# Audit Report Summary

The summary should describe how the audit was conducted, including the sequence of processes that were assessed. The details of each process will come later in the report. Also included should be a comment about any processes that could not be observed and whether the lapse affected the ability to achieve the audit objective. This may result in, for example, a caveat to a supplier qualification: "The supplier is provisionally qualified based upon evidence available, but a further visit will be required in six months to assess the clean room process."

There should be a brief mention of the number of findings, including how they were graded: major, minor, observation, or opportunity for improvement.

Finally, the summary should conclude with the recommendation. A company is recommended for continued certification to a standard such as ISO 13485 or a supplier should have its status upgraded from provisional to fully qualified. This statement relates directly back to the objective of the audit.

The summary is followed by detailed information about each process. This section of the report should encompass all the documents that were reviewed, the individuals interviewed (either by name or function, depending on your organization's established procedures), and the evidence that was assessed. It's essential to be thorough. The bar is set higher due to the remote conditions. The assumption is that it's easier to deceive an auditor or to misrepresent the level of control of a process because standard tools of observation have been either curtailed or obviated.

List all the bits of evidence that were assessed. If appropriate, note any request for additional samples. As with any other audit report, make note of benchmarked practices. Comment on your ability to reasonably verify the conformance and effectiveness of a process. Mention items such as:

- Raw materials certifications match the lot numbers recorded on the production routers.
- Drawing revision levels on purchase orders match those found in the engineering files.

- Customer orders are aligned with quotations and production routers.

In all instances, this allows the auditor to demonstrate that:
- The audit was conducted in accordance with the process approach.
- The risks that might have affected the auditor's ability to conduct the audit have been addressed and mitigated.
- There is adequate objective evidence to substantiate the audit conclusion.
- The audit client should have confidence that the audit objective has been achieved.

---

# Findings

The final section in the audit report is the findings. As with any report, each should be noted separately. To be complete, a finding should have three components: the nonconformance, the standard, and the evidence. For example: "There is no evidence that in-process inspections have been conducted for work orders 78-336 and 78-402. The requirements are found in procedure SP 837-41 Rev. G." Even though this evidence has been previously detailed earlier in the report, it is essential to include it in the finding. This highlights the fact that the finding is based on objective evidence.

In a remote auditing scenario, the risk of having a finding challenged may be heightened. This is due to no other reason than the auditee may think that the remote nature of the audit resulted in misunderstanding of the evidence presented. This is the rationale for ensuring that large and representative samples are obtained. It mitigates any suggestion that the samples used were anomalous or not reflective of the process.

Distribute the report in accordance with your procedures.

# CHAPTER EIGHT

# Follow-Up and Future Planning

The auditor should follow up as with any other audit. Typical activities might be a debrief with the audit client to reiterate any recommendation. There will be housekeeping activities such as posting the report in the system, scheduling the next audit, logging any nonconformances into the database, and emailing the auditee to remind them of required actions.

Now that the audit report has been posted, it's time to purge the proprietary information that was used during the audit. It's important to be thorough. There is an inherent liability for any breach of security or disclosure of confidential information resulting from a failure to adequately dispose of the documentation.

Likely candidates to check include:

- Computer files
- Documents parked on your computer's desktop
- Images on your smart phone
- Emails (including those threaded conversations that may replicate the information)
- Hard copies of documents that were printed to facilitate interviews

There may be a compelling reason to retain a document. This could be the case if it has significant information that supports an audit finding. However, any signed agreement that says the document is required to be destroyed trumps your need. Make some notes and dispose of the document.

Plan for anticipated corrective action responses. It's not uncommon for follow-ups to corrective actions to be done completely remotely. So, there's no big change here. This is especially true for minor nonconformances.

However, if there was a major finding, you may choose to plan a follow-up visit. This could be either remote or on-site. That takes us back to the assessment of risk. Can the auditor reliably confirm effective implementation of a corrective action plan to address a major nonconformance? What are the risks of doing it remotely? Either way, a visit needs to be scheduled.

There should be an assessment of the audit process. The feedback you requested from the auditee is a valuable input to this evaluation. Topics for consideration might relate to the following:

- Extent to which the audit objective was achieved
- Auditor's familiarity and competence with remote auditing activities
- Constraints that limited the availability of sufficient evidence
- Problems that arose:
  o Individuals not accessible despite scheduling and notification
  o Information and communication technology issues:
    ▪ Weak internet connection
    ▪ Dropped web conferencing call
    ▪ Screen sharing not allowed due to undisclosed security protocols
    ▪ Limited information from webcam due to individuals' lack of familiarity with equipment
  o Auditee's discomfort with remote interviewing

Based upon the results of the assessment, it will be appropriate to take action. These actions will address additional risks, resource requirements, and opportunities to improve that have been identified. Potential actions include:

- Revert to on-site audit for an auditee.
- Plan for additional auditor training.
- Review and determine if there needs to be a change to the method and content of communication with auditee prior to audit.
- Adjust future audit plans considering what has been learned.

It's important to note that the audit schedule should be reviewed periodically and revised. The circumstances that prompted the need for a remote audit—such as the COVID-19 pandemic—may have abated. Or review of the results of audits may suggest that there are too many gaps in the information to ensure the reliability of the process. And, there are all the usual reasons to revisit the audit schedule. Things change. New products get introduced. Volume increases. A second shift gets added. Key personnel leave or are re-assigned. A new ERP system gets installed. An international standard is revised. All of these factors affect your quality management system and subsequently your audit program.

Auditing, just like any other process, has a complete plan-do-check-act (PDCA) cycle. The audits are planned and then conducted. The steps discussed in this chapter relate to the "C" and "A" of the cycle. We check to determine the outcome of the process. Based on the information gained, we take action. And, afterward, we plan for the next round of audits.

# CHAPTER NINE

# Conclusion

It should be clear that remote auditing is not a new category of audits. It's the same first-, second-, and third-party audits that we've been accustomed to for the last several decades. Back in the early 1990s most documented information was still in paper form. The internet was in its infancy, phones hadn't become smart yet, and robotics industries were predominantly futuristic. Little of the technology that enables remote auditing practices today existed outside of engineering labs.

Things change.

It is appropriate for auditors to adjust their audit practices to be aligned with the tools that the auditees are now using to operate. Auditors need to hone these skills. They need to:

- Develop the ability and the agility to recognize changes that affect their audit process.
- Assess risks when planning to use remote auditing tools.
- Learn about the information and communications technology tools that are available to them.
- Ensure they have the necessary training to conduct audits using remote auditing practices.
- Create audit schedules with consideration of the pros and cons of using remote auditing tools.
- Incorporate these new tools into their audit plans.

- Learn how to optimize the new technologies to improve the audit outcomes.
- Be vigilant regarding confidentiality and security risks and constraints.
- Communicate with the auditee to ensure a mutually successful audit experience.
- Monitor their program for whatever the next changes will bring.

# Bibliography

International Organization for Standardization. (2018). *Guidelines for auditing management systems* (ISO Standard No. 19011).

*ISO 9001 Auditing Practices Group Guidance on Remote Audits.* (April 2020).

Robitaille, Denise. *9 Keys to Successful Audits*. Chico: Paton Professional, 2014.

# Index

## ABOUT THE AUTHOR

Denise Robitaille has authored a dozen books, including: *The 9 Keys to Successful Audits*. She is chair of ISO/PC 302, the project committee that revised the ISO 19011, Guidelines for auditing management systems, standard.

Denise is an active member of the ISO/TC 176 Auditing Practices Group that develops papers providing guidance on auditing. She has participated internationally in standards development for more than 18 years. Denise is a Fellow of the American Society for Quality and an Exemplar Global certified lead auditor.

She is internationally recognized for her work and is a frequent speaker at conferences.

She continues to help companies achieve ISO 9001 registration and to improve their quality management systems.

Made in United States
Orlando, FL
27 February 2022